Travel Snapshots

IRELAND

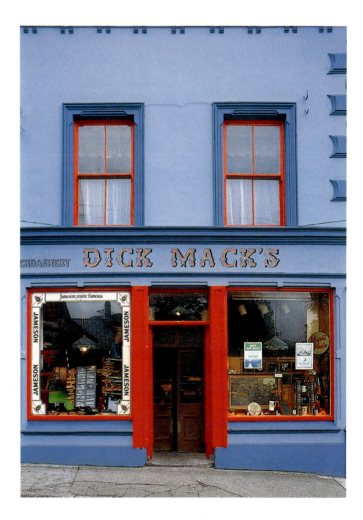

Text
Simona Tarchetti

Photographs
Guilio Veggi

Graphic design
Patrizia Balocco

Contents

Landscapes and legends .... *page 32*
A city on a human scale .... *page 62*
A Celtic stronghold .... *page 94*

2-3 *The Cliffs of Moher, one of the most imposing natural sights in Ireland, rise up like a wall for almost 600 feet and stretch for 5 miles along the western coast of Ireland.*

4-5- *A picture of the typical landscape of the Dingle peninsula. The predominant green of the countryside contrasts with a sky which is often misty and laden with clouds.*

6-7 *In the charming area of Connemara, in the far west of the country, the imposing Abbey of Kylemore is reflected in the clear waters of the lake on whose shores it stands.*

8 *The barren and windswept Dingle peninsula, the most westerly point in the country, reaches out into the ocean.*

9 *To the north of Cong, in County Galway, lies Ashford Castle, a large manor house with crenellated towers, built in 1870.*

10-11 *Red hair and freckly cheeks are a characteristic feature of the Irish.*

12-13 *The tables of a typical Irish pub are normally laden with full glasses of the national drink, a dark stout produced by Guinness.*

14-15 *The River Liffey flows through the center of Dublin and over the course of the centuries many bridges have been built to link the two parts of the city.*

16-17 *Clifden Town is the most important town in Connemara, a wild and often desolate region in the county of Galway.*

Published in North America by
AAA Publishing
1000 AAA Drive
Heathrow, Florida 32746
www.aaa.com

© 1993 White Star S.r.l.
Via Candido Sassone, 22/24
13100 Vercelli, Italy
www.whitestar.it

ISBN 1-56251-810-0
123456 0605040302

Printed in Singapore
Color separations by Magenta Lit. Con., Singapore

Introduction

Ireland really is the Emerald Isle. This is a fascinating and verdant country, where the passage of time is marked by the hooves of a horse trotting along a winding road, and where the changeable and capricious sky forms a splendid backdrop to the gently sloping, velvety hills and green pastures dotted with grazing animals. On this island at the extreme western end of Europe, the colours of nature have a particular intensity: the shades of green - the predominant colour - are ever-changing, while the blues, filtering through whirling puffs of clouds, are soft pastels over the crests of the hills, or clearer hues in the beautiful contrast between the steep coastal cliffs and the foaming ocean. The Atlantic climate does not offer great extremes of hot and cold and the climate is generally mild, albeit wet. Along the Atlantic coast, in the period between December and March, the average monthly temperature is 44°F, while, in the east, it is slightly lower, at around 42°F. Thus, in sheltered valleys, such as those around Killarney, there is a rich evergreen vegetation which includes laurels, rhododendrons, the Mediterranean arbutus, oak, holly and other deciduous trees. In December and January, sheltered gardens in Dublin often still have an abundance of blooms. In any case, be it because of the dark threatening clouds or the veil of mist on the horizon, the weather is an integral part of the beauty of the Irish landscape.

The glaciers of the quaternary period were principally responsible for the morphology of the island with raised coasts overlooking the sea and "mountains" which are seldom more than 2000 feet high. The highest point in the island is Carrantuohill in the range known as Macgillycuddy's Reeks, in Kerry, which reaches a height of 3,414 feet. In the west, the island has no defences against the wind blowing in from the Atlantic and causes much damage to standing crops, especially when accompanied by heavy rains. In the east, the large, inner plain facing the Irish Sea is like a natural gateway to nearby Great Britain. The life of this people of stock-raisers and farmers is deeply rooted in the green pastures, desolate bogs, and uncultivated heath

that cover almost one fifth of the island. They are farmers, and their harsh and stubborn character has been formed by an ungenerous land and a troubled history. The ancient traces of pre-Christian invaders and the very position of the island have contributed to give this island people a flourishing cultural vivacity and a human temperament which is as changeable as the colours of the sky. The sense of the past is still very much alive in the memories of this people.

Despite 20th-century urbanization, Irish society is primarily rural and attached to melancholy peat bogs, where silence and loneliness capture the imagination of foreign visitors, and reveal the love these people feel for nature, open spaces, and the myths and legends of their antique land. Few other countries have had such a turbulent past as Ireland whose origins are shrouded in the mists of time and yet here, the past is an ever-present companion. This past has left an indelible mark and many of the folk traditions can be traced back to Celtic religious rites and the legends surrounding the miracles performed by St. Patrick. This restless race, which has maintained and strengthened its own diversity despite endless periods of foreign rule, shows a remarkable capability of bringing the past into the present. This conflicting and elusive character, embodied by "the Tinkers", Ireland's last nomads, suddenly bursts forth in all its theatricality during lively discussions in pubs and in arguments among groups of farmers at cattle markets. Today's Irishman is as obstinate and generous as his ancestors, the "Firbolg" who, with immense patience, built the megalithic tumuli at Newgrange in the Boyne valley, and in more ancient times, the Neolithic settlements found near Lough Gur, in County Limerick.

During their expansion across Europe, the Celts arrived in Ireland, where they settled. Like their forebears on the continent, the Celts in Ireland established themselves in small states. Their constitution was completely monarchic and each state was ruled over by an elected leader who bore the name of king. Each state, however small, strove to achieve and maintain political independence, but this often proved impracticable and for self-protection, the smaller states formed into groups which accepted the hegemony of a superior king. The tall, blond Gaels lived on the island until the fifth century, building a single Celtic nation and passing down the unmistakable and unique features and the charming cultural elements that are fully appreciated and even slightly envied in western countries today. Welsh, Scottish and Irish Gaelic, as well as the idiom of the Bretons all derive from the language of this people. In Ireland, this ancient language survived both Christianization and subsequent foreign rule. The fact

18 *The interior of the elegant and modern St. Stephen's Green shopping centre with an enormouns circular glass clock.*

19 top *St Stephen's Green Centre, with its shops, boutiques, art galleries and antique dealers, is built on the edge of the public park of the-same name in the centre of the city.*

19 bottom *The Dubliners frequently visit the city's cafes where they can enjoy a piece of apple tart with cream.*

20-21 *The Gothic St. Patrick's Cathedral in Dublin was begun in the 12th century and became the chief cathedral of the Irish Protestant Church during English dominion.*

22-23 *St. Stephen's Green is a green oasis in the centre of the city where one can relax. In spring and summer many newly-weds come here to have their wedding photographs taken.*

that it remained unchanged in the course of time is also perhaps due to the fact that the Romans did not invade the island. This harmonious and musical language is, together with the Roman Catholic religion, a symbol of national identity. It has been the official language of the Republic of Ireland since 1921, and is a compulsory subject at school. However, the Irish language is written and spoken only by a small percentage of the population; the so-called Irish speakers, who nowadays number about 75,000-80,000 and are concentrated in a few wild and lonely areas of the country: the seven districts in the extreme western and northern counties called An Gaeltacht (Gael's Land) which is distinguished by the fact that its roadsigns are red. The decline in the use of the language was caused both by the spread of English and the emigration brought about by the great famine which followed the potato blight in the 1840's. Many great Irish writers such as Joyce, Shaw, and Yeats wrote in English, but their "exotic" style immediately revealed their Irish origins. In ancient times, the nascent Irish race was the most isolated of European cultures. This Celtic population was completely cut off for centuries and it was not affected by the Roman influence which had such a great effect on mainland Europe and neighbouring Great Britain. As in transalpine Gaul and other parts of Britain, Druidism was widespread in Ireland during the Celtic domination. Druids were a sort of class of wise men who claimed to be experts in all the higher branches of knowledge. They professed to know about the gods, the afterlife, the movement of the planets and stars and were accepted as authorities in matters of religion and law. Even after the conversion of Ireland to Christianity, they continued their function as soothsayers and wise men.

St. Patrick, who reached the island in A.D. 432, opened the way to the word of God. Celtic chronicles and myths mingled with Christian tales, forming the rich substratum of pagan superstition and Catholic tradition that is still so deeply rooted in the minds of the common people. Prominent among the scholarly and uniquely beautiful testimonies of this early Christian period are the Book of Durrow and the Book of Kells, exquisitely illuminated manuscripts produced by Irish monks. These give us an idea of what this early period of Christianity was like as well as informing us about Irish legends, Gaelic heroes and sagas of elves, wizards, and fairies. The Irish themselves still hand down these rich stories, in which religious events are mixed with fanciful tales. On Croagh Patrick, the sacred mountain of Ireland, myths and legends are recalled every year when thousands of pilgrims join in a religious procession and climb to the top to pray to St. Patrick so that he might intervene on behalf of the penitents. The old Celtic feast of Lughnasa was also celebrated on this spot and during this feast, the ancient Druids prayed and made propitiatory offerings to obtain good harvests.

St. Patrick, Ireland's Patron Saint, is given the credit for the conversion of the island to Christianity. The people remained faithful to their beliefs even during periods of barbarian rule, when first the Danes, then the Normans attacked the monasteries and burned the religious settlements. In the ninth century, the Vikings settled on the island, striking terror into the hearts of the natives by their burning and pillaging. Numerous coastal villages, which later developed into cities such as Dublin, Wicklow, Arklow, Cork, and Limerick, were originally the home ports of Viking longships and it was from here that the Norsemen set out on their raids towards the inner parts of the country. To defend themselves, the Irish built many circular towers, which were impregnable, fifteen - foot - high fortresses, and the remains of which still stand in Ardmore, Glendalough, and Clonmacnois.

Viking rule marked the end of Irish isolation and the growth of human settlements along the coast increased trade and connections with Europe. However, together with commercial traffic, new cultural influences reached the island and Ireland began to play an increasingly active role in the political and religious rivalries of the other European countries, particularly neighboring England. Norman adventurers, such as Strongbow, came ashore looking for new lands and possessions. Unlike the Vikings, the Normans went further inland, to the uplands, gradually fortifying the newly conquered areas with imposing turreted castles whose walls were more than fifteen feet thick. Moreover, they built special structures called "tower-house castles" which had a clearly defensive function. Today, these are lonely ruins overlooking the coast from the top of promontories, and they stand out against the green landscape of the island, making it more melancholy. Blarney Castle with its famous stone of eloquence, Bunratty Castle in County Clare, surrounded by a wonderful park, and the great Anglo-Norman fortification of Trim are only a few of the best preserved tower-houses among the hundreds built on Irish territory. Together with the Normans, numerous monastic orders settled in the island, and during the following three centuries, they devoted themselves to preaching and spreading the Christian faith, reinforcing in this way the foundations of that deep, sometimes fanatical, religious sense which has had such a great influence on Irish history.

Dublin bears the marks of Norman rule more

clearly than other cities; examples are St. Patrick's and Christchurch cathedrals which now belong to the Protestant Church of Ireland. The former, founded by Strongbow in 1172, was largely rebuilt in the last century when the Gothic style came into favour once more. Dublin Castle, also of Norman origin, was the bulwark and symbol of English rule until 1920. It was begun at the start of the 13th century and enlarged and remodelled more than once. Until the Elizabethan age, English rule was limited to the coastal region known as "The Pale", which extended from Dundalk as far as Dublin Bay. However, after the defeat of the Irish army by William of Orange in the battle of the Boyne in 1690, the sovereignty of the British Parliament was firmly established in the whole island. During the 18th century, Dublin experienced a period of splendid urban growth and the present-day appearance of some parts of the city date back to this period. The oldest part of the city was destroyed, and in its place, many Georgian style buildings were erected. Wide boulevards like O'Connell, Upper Merton and Baggot Street were laid out, and bridges and large squares were built. The inevitable uniformity of the buildings erected in this style induced Dubliners to transform the front entrances of their plain houses into ornamental works, the famous "Doors of Dublin", which, with their bright colours and harmonious shapes, are expressions of the irreverent individual creativity always present in the Irish soul.

The city bears evident marks of both past and recent troubles; on O'Connell Street, on the facade of the General Post Office, one can see bullet holes dating back to 1916, when a group of bold, idealistic patriots tried to take possession of the building and started a popular insurrection that ended in tragedy. St. Mary's Pro-Cathedral, the city's main Roman Catholic church was built on the left bank of the Liffey between 1815 and 1825. At that period this was on the outskirts of the city but pressure from the Protestant community and strict anti-Catholic laws in force at the time prevented it being built in the centre of the city. The fact that the two Protestant churches of Christchurch and St.Patrick's are in such splendidly central positions compared to St. Mary's bears witness to the repression which the Catholics in Ireland had to suffer for centuries in a country where they represented 95% of the population. Today, Dublin contains nearly 700 churches and chapels built to satisfy the needs of the densely-populated local archdiocese. Moreover, there are 276 convents and 108 religious institutions, which play leading roles in the management of social, educational, and health services.

Ancient Dublin was founded by Scandinavian Vikings in a wonderful natural location in a wide valley overlooked by gentle hills. Facing the large bay at the mouth of the river Liffey, the city became an active centre for trade with nearby England and the rest of Europe. The vitality of the Irish capital can be found in the pages of Joyce's *Ulysses*. The main character of this novel, Leopold Bloom, is still remembered every year on June 16th "Bloomsday", when young actors in period costumes recite passages and soliloquies from Joyce's work in the streets of the city. The capital city is one of the most prolific breeding grounds for new ideas and many writers of genius have their roots here. These include Jonathan Swift, biting and sarcastic in his satire; John Millington Synge, who wrote of the hard, Irish daily life; Sean O'Casey and, of course, Joyce himself. Oliver Goldsmith, Oscar Wilde, Bram Stoker (author of *Dracula*), and Samuel Beckett all studied at Trinity College, which was founded by Elizabeth I in 1592 as the Irish equivalent of Oxford and Cambridge Universities. Here, one can visit the famous Old Library, where the Book of Kells and other ancient manuscripts are displayed in the Long Room. These manuscripts are all wonderfully illuminated by Irish monks and are considered to be true art treasures of the High Middle Ages.

Some 800 pubs are scattered throughout the city. In these places, gallons of beer are consumed, litres of whiskey are sipped, and floods of words are spent in animated talks and heated debates which sometimes end with the singing of patriotic songs. Dublin pubs have been a meeting place for the young and the old, for men and women. Glasses are filled with classic Irish stout atop of which the foam forms a thick layer through which the dark liquid is then sipped. In Ireland, the most commonly drunk beer is Guinness, which has been produced and marketed in the country since 1779. The great dynasty of master-brewers was founded twenty years earlier by Arthur Guinness who produced ale in a small brewery in St. James Gate, before introducing the darker porter to Ireland in 1779. Today, almost eighty per cent of Irish barley is used for the production of Guinness. The typical bitter taste and gentle, sweetish aftertaste does not derive from the brewing process, which is similar for all types of beer, but from the fact that part of the barley used during the fermentation is previously roasted. In Irish pubs, pints of beer are pulled with religious slowness to avoid producing too much froth. A regular Guinness drinker first appreciates the colour of the brew and then drinks it in long, satisfying gulps. Pubs in Dublin still retain the traditional dark wood furniture. Some of them are elegantly finished in mahogany and brass; others have a more casual look, with hard stools, and old mirrors on the walls. Most of them, however, have a comfortable half-light and an atmosphere of domestic privacy that fosters conversation and mutual acquaintance. "Pub

crawling", a pilgrimage from one pub to the other, is a custom still kept alive by first-year students at Dublin University and it is also practised by some tourists as a way of exploring and discovering the varied universe of Dublin's pubs. The "Brazen Head" boasts the oldest liquor licence in Ireland, and the historical "Davy Byrne's" is mentioned in Joyce's *Ulysses*. Musicians meet at "O'Donoghues" in Merrion Row, while horse racing fans and sportsmen frequent the "Old Stand".

Dublin is a town where you can feel the past living in the present. On the one hand, remarkable restoration work on the Custom House, built in 1781-91 by the ingenious architect James Gordon, is being carried out, while new and very modern buildings rise up in the ambitious financial centre. A variety of ancient and renowned bookshops such as Hodges Figgis, Greene's and Fred Hanna's stand ready to satisfy every request of the Dubliners. The Irish have a real and ardent passion for horses and the Smithfield Horse Market takes place in a densely populated suburb in the north of the city on the first Sunday of every month. Moving out of the capital, one enters a wonderful world of unlimited expanses of grass, steep fjords, long, desolate stretches of beach, wild moors, Norman towers rising from the mist and crumbling castles.

Further to the north, in an area between the Irish Sea and the Boyne River, one can relive the history of the country by visiting the ancient monastery of Kells, although only a few high crosses and a circular tower still remain. From the hill of Tara, the royal residence of the Celts, one can admire the graves and the earthworks where the Gaelic Kings and priests gathered their clans, while in Newgrange, one can travel back into prehistory when visiting the huge, 40-foot-high Neolithic burial chamber, an imposing reminder of the cult of the dead that still survives today. The physical characteristics of the island are essentially influenced by the geology of the land; the northern coasts, made up mostly of granite or other magma rocks, have rough and steep outlines, while, along the southwestern edge, the geologically younger systems of sandstone and limestone have produced more uneven coastal outlines, with fjords and deep creeks. Along the Atlantic coast, the indented coastline is lapped by the warm waters of the Gulf Stream, which contributes to the damp and foggy climate. The mild winters and the cool summers facilitate the vigorous growth of trees, meadows, and multi-coloured shrubs which flower from April to October.

The counties of Cork and Kerry represent the pure and hard heart of Ireland, where people's souls live in symbiosis with the secret rhythm of the land and with an irascible sky filled with clouds. Here, in southwestern Ireland, the beauty of nature becomes predominant; the island extends into five peninsulas

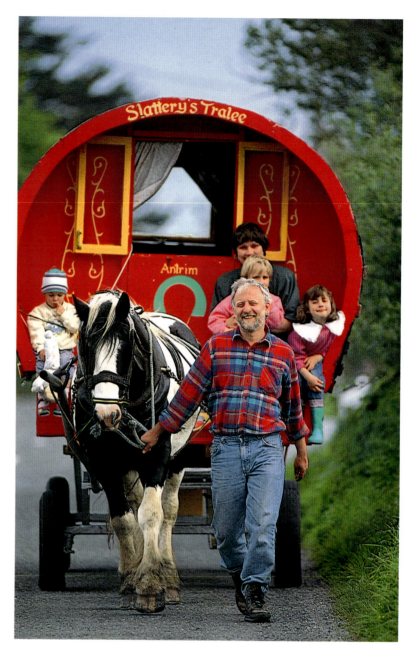

24 *The typical painted horse cart pulled by a single horse was once used by Irish nomads and is now used by tourists whio wich to enjoy an alternative sort of holiday.*

like fingers outstretched into the Atlantic, each with its own unforgettable scenery. Beaches alternate with rocky spurs and the winding roads are flanked by charming stretches of green brightened by fuchsias, rhododendrons, palm trees, and agaves. From Mizen Head promontory, one can enjoy the unique sight of the ocean roaring into deep ravines below the vertical cliffs. It is easy to see how, over the centuries, many ships have been wrecked here, flung by the violent waves against these steep rocks that are so often hidden by a thick fog. The charm of Dunmanus Bay is in sharp contrast to the rough and barren land surrounding it. Indeed, the land is so poor that the primary food source of the inhabitants of this area has always been the sea. Along the Ring of Kerry, the most famous itinerary through the Iveragh peninsula, one can admire the highest mountains on the whole island, covered with moors and sparkling with trout-rich streams. One can also admire the many lakes around Killarney. The Dingle peninsula is more charming and wild and is the most western tip of Ireland; narrow roads wind lazily to the top of the cliffs, from which one can see the bare and windswept outlines of the surrounding mountains or the rocky spurs of the Blasket Islands.

One will experience very different emotions upon visiting the traditional horse market held at Killorglin in County Kerry, where merchants and buyers, once the negotiations on the price of the animal have finished, seal the newly reached agreement with a vigorous handshake and mark the back of the sold animal with a fistful of mud.

During the first week of August, an unusual celebration called Puck Fair takes place in the same town. The origins of this event probably go back to Celtic fertility rites and to the worship of Pan, the goat-legged heathen God. During this feast, a wild billy goat is crowned King of Ireland for three days. On the occasion of this pageant an important cattle market is held and local agricultural products are sold. The streets of the town are enlivened by stalls and kiosks, while pubs are allowed to stay open into the early hours. During these three days and nights of cheerful merrymaking, Killorglin is a destination of the caravans of the last Irish nomads, the Tinkers, who meet in one place at least once a year. The ancestors of these tireless travellers are not related at all to Rom gypsies or to other gypsy tribes on the continent. On the contrary, it is generally believed that the Irish nomad group descends from ancient indigenous people who separated from civilized society, preferring continuous wandering to the sedentary life in the villages. The Tinkers used to move across the island in brightly coloured horse-drawn carts, the women wrapped in woollen shawls. The menfolk used a

25 *As a result of the demographic explosion which has taken place in the last 25 years, almost 50% of the population is younger than 25.*

special secret language called Shelta to communicate among themselves but this language has been almost completely lost. The economic activity of these gypsies was of particular importance in the rural society of the time; essentially, it consisted of mending tools, tinning copper pots, selling junk, and trading in animals. Today, because of increasing changes in Irish society and progressive agricultural mechanization, the few remaining wandering families prefer to live near inhabited areas, where they establish settlements made of shacks.

Among the most famous and frequently photographed landscapes of the island are the imposing cliffs of Moher in County Clare, 5 miles long and rising vertically from the ocean for 600 feet. From O'Brien's Tower, the impressive view is really unforgettable. As the sun's rays hit the cliffs they change colour during the course of the day, whereas at sunset, the bare rock is bathed in a warm, golden light. Also in County Clare, a very special area can be found along a short stretch of the coast going down to Galway Bay. This territory, completely dry on the surface, appears to be made up of deeply cracked platforms of grey calcareous stone, by furrowed fields, and by shallow holes. This "lunar" landscape is known as the Burren, a quadrilateral, seemingly barren area covered with stones but which contains a hidden botanical and geological paradise. In the underground passages and in the hollows dug out in the subsoil, the percolating water has created a strange system of stalactites and stalagmites, constructed in the course of a million years by the slow, concentric sedimentation of small alabaster crystals. In narrow clefts and in those areas where there is a little soil, this area conceals a unique biota in which typically Mediterranean species grow alongside Alpine plants and specimens of Arctic flora. In spite of the poor and scrubby vegetative covering and the desolation of the present-day landscape, the Burren was once covered with vigorous forests and inhabited by primitive people, who erected many stone tombs, among which is the famous dolmen of Poulnabrone. Prehistoric ruins and ancient traces of human industry appear on the horizon like gigantic sleeping animals resting in the gloomy landscape.

The rugged peninsula of Connaught, embracing Galway, Mayo, Sligo, Leitrim, and Roscommon, appears barren and wild in the far-western area near the ocean, where steep mountains, silent plains, and barren moors prevail; on the contrary, the eastern area, which stretches as far as the Shannon, is more productive and densely populated, with green pastures and tilled fields. Connaught is also a reminder of the suffering of the Irish people; today, throughout the area, you can still see the ruins of the

26 Along the beautiful coasts of County Kerry, rocky stretches alternate with low sandy shorelines.

27 top In Connemara the widespread use of horses is favoured by the abundance of meadows suitable for grazing.

27 centre A bucolic image of the county of Galway. According to Irish traditions and legends which are very widespread in this area, the first inhabitant of the island was a horse.

27 bottom Some parts of the Aran Islands, opposite Galway Bay, are uninhabited because of the nature of the land which is often boggy and not very fertile. In the picture, a typical Irish pony and a donkey graze near a farmhouse.

28-29 Dunguaire Castle stands in a picturesque position dominating Galway Bay. This manor, dating from the 15th century, has been carefully restored and houses a precious collection of historical and literary importance.

30-31 The more westerly counties of Ireland and County Kerry in particular, are continuously swept by winds blowing in from the Atlantic and enjoy the beneficial effects of the Gulf Stream.

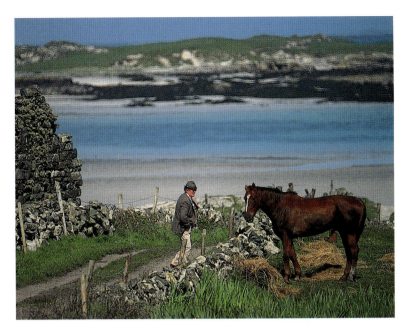

deserted houses in the middle of the fields where people used to grow potatoes. With the Great Famine, which began in the autumn of 1845 and caused a million deaths from starvation, the town of Galway became the main harbour from which thousands of people sailed on dreary, emigrant ships toward new, American frontiers. Yet these barren moors, in spite of their solitude, are filled with an emotional warmth that permeates the soul of the inhabitants, while the scent of moss hovers over the damp peat bogs and the pungent alcoholic smell of poteen rises from the clandestine distilleries of Lattermore, Lattermullen, and Rosmuck.

The Gaeltacht of Connemara, one of the last traditional strongholds of Gaelic culture, begins at the edges of County Galway, when suddenly one sees road signs written only in Irish with no translation into English. Since the 1970's, the area has been designated the National Park of Connemara in order to protect at least a part of the bog. This is an uncultivated and marshy meadow that had been exploited for years as grazing land and as a source of peat, which was used as fuel. Since it was declared a protected area, Connaught has become a tourist region; the sweet slopes of the Twelve Pins, the lonely moors of Maan Cross, and the amazing lakes of Lough Corrib and Lough Conn are the perfect backdrop for those who love fishing, solitary excursions on mountains bikes, and horse riding. One can go pony-trekking on one of the famous Connemara ponies.

For those who appreciate the vestiges of ancient Celtic and early Christian beginnings, the historical and artistic route winds along the shores of the lakes. Travelling this route, one reaches Ross Emily Abbey, a huge Franciscan monastery; Cong Abbey, a beautiful example of Romanesque and Irish style; Kylemore Abbey, an imposing building of granite and limestone that houses a college run by Benedictine nuns; and finally, the isle of Inishmore, where one can admire Dun Aengus, the stately fortification whose concentric walls were built on the edge of the cliff. County Mayo is the scene of a great religious festival on the last Sunday in July when thousands of pilgrims flock to the base of the holy mountain Croagh Patrick, from which, according to tradition, St. Patrick threw the snakes which infested the island into the sea. In reality, snakes have never existed in Ireland, but, from the story, one understands that these reptiles are metaphors for pagan symbols and the ancient temptations of the Irish who were newly converted. From the top of the mountain, one has a wonderful view of the Atlantic with the underlying Clew Bay and the small off-shore islands. The irregular outline of Achill Island, the widest Irish island, linked to the mainland by a bridge, can sometimes be seen in the distance. The northernmost part of the country, after the desolate moor of Erris marsh, is dominated by a wonderful combination of dizzying cliffs, golden beaches, moors of purple heather, and small, square, straw-roofed cottages surrounded by long, winding walls that enclose grazing animals and small fields. In order to bring to life the lines by William Butler Yeats, who loved the sweet and sleepy county of Sligo (where he is buried, near the small church of Drumcliff), it would be necessary to explore the small lake of Glencare, the extraordinary Benbulben Mountain, the surroundings of the Lough Gill, whose isle, Inisfree, inspired a famous poem, and the imposing Lissadell House, situated at the northern end of Drumcliff Bay. This region is still rich in that beauty which the reader can experience in the verses of this poet who won the Nobel prize for literature in 1923. This region also contains Carrowmore, one of the largest megalithic graves in Europe, and the old port of Rosses Point, where a great number of emigrant ships departed for New York. Moreover, one can admire the long beaches of Mullaghmore and Streedagh Point, where four Spanish galleons were shipwrecked, and the grim, mysterious Clocknarea, on whose slopes Maeve, the warrior queen of Celtic mythology, was buried.

The county of Donegal, like Connaught, was almost completely ignored by English settlers, and for this reason, the traditions and the Gaelic-Irish language have been preserved here. From an economic and social point of view, these are backward regions, and wild, northwestern Ireland still offers unspoilt areas, silent mountain valleys, deserted beaches, and small villages situated on the slopes of hills. Donegal town can be considered an entrance to this wild region overlooking the Atlantic, where the main roads from Sligo, Londonderry, and western Donegal converge. A lively market takes place in Diamond Square; beside the stalls offering fresh fish every day, there are the typical shops selling the famous tweed articles. This very strong fabric is still hand-woven in the numerous houses of the town. It is then used to make hats, jackets, and cloaks whose dark colours remind one of the colours of the heather on the moors, the black turf, the low, damp fog, and the leaden sky with its stormy clouds. The region of Donegal has many original characteristics: it does not have the deep, irregular inlets of the southwestern part of Ireland nor does it have the sweet hills of Kerry. The wonderful steep cliffs of Slieve League and the ancient mountains which are the natural continuation of the Scottish highlands, have been shaped from the hard granite rock which is the typical rock type in this northwestern county.

The Inishowen Peninsula, in the northernmost

part of Ireland, has a charming landscape because of its unspoiled and wild nature; the desolate region culminates in Malin Head, a tongue stretching out into the sea, from which one can admire one of the most beautiful views in the country: the ocean, as far as the eye can see. The main town in the area is Buncrana, which overlooks the long and narrow Lough Swilly. However, tourists prefer the neat and austere village called Malin with its small, white cottages whose thatched roofs are tied down with strong ropes which are fixed to the walls in order to protect them from the raging Atlantic wind. What makes Donegal so charming is undoubtedly the force of nature, which has shaped and reinforced the link between the inhabitants and their environment. The latter is governed by the rules dictated by the sea and by the slow passing of the seasons that are sometimes fertile and sometimes barren. The outpost of Donegal is the hilly island of Arranmore which is served by ferry boats which ply to and from Burtonport every hour. Arranmore has nice, small beaches, rocky promontories, lonely coastal ravines, small fields surrounded by walls, and scattered white houses.

The other numerous islands along the Irish coast have unique peculiarities, valiantly defended by the small communities who occupy them and who want to preserve their natural beauty. They are surviving hermitages, where time has not diminished the most striking customs and the ancient, rural rites and ways of fishing. Their existence is linked to the survival of the Gaelic language, traditions, mysteries, ballads, and village festivals. The Aran Islands appear as three irregular shapes emerging from the sea across from Galway Bay; they contain many remains of prehistoric fortresses, medieval towers, small early Christian churches, and holy fountains. Irishmore, Inishmaan, and Inisheer seem to be made entirely of stones, with which the inhabitants built a great many low walls used to protect small plots of land and scanty crops from the wind. The legendary Aran Islands fired the imaginations of many writers and artists: during the Gaelic Renaissance, J. M. Synge was inspired by the primitive and unchanged charm of these pearls of calcareous rock emerging from the vast ocean, to write some of his better works.

Skellig Michael is an island situated seven miles from the coast, opposite the Iveragh peninsula in County Kerry, but it is often isolated from the world when the sea becomes stormy. The ruins of an ancient early Christian monastery are perched on its rocky slopes. The ruins of the buildings and of the two chapels, with their capsized-keel-shaped roofs, are situated on several ledges which skillful monks created on a plateau about 500 feet above sea level. The uninterrupted crash of the waves, the cries of seabirds, and the howling of the wind are the only sounds you can hear in this lonely place. But from the ninth to the twelfth or thirteenth century, Skellig Michael was home to a dozen monks who lived in pious isolation on these steep rocks. The site still has a certain religious charm, even if today the only occasional visitors to the small island are tourists looking for an exciting trip to a magic place where time seems to have stood still.

In an ideal vision of Ireland, one can see how the history and customs of the people always centre around the supernatural and the fantastic. The reserved and wild nature of the island, with its enchanting green expanses and its romantic, bright sky, easily conjures up the magic, fairy-tale notes of Irish legends and stories.

Landscapes and Legends

The Irish landscape is particularly attractive because of its variety. In some areas of the extreme west, it is wild and desolate while in other areas there are clear signs of ancient human presence. Historical events have moulded the people of this island in the same way as a river models the valley in which it flows.

The series of plateaux which form the continental shelf were profoundly modified by erosion caused by glaciers during the ice age. The low mountains of northern Ireland and the gently sloping coastal hills are the result of ancient rocks which have been moulded in the course of time. The ocean has eaten into and shaped the coastline with all its force, creating a great variety of different types of shore. The appearance of the landscape changes with the passage of the clouds and one is constantly transported back in time as one discovers remains of paleochristian churches which blend into the greenery of the countryside or ruins of castles on the shores of lakes or in the midst of a plain.

32 top *The charming Dingle peninsula in County Kerry has a particularly wild beauty and contains steep cliffs, sandy bays and heather-covered hills.*

32 bottom *The curious geometry of the basalt columns of the Giant's Causeway, in Northern Ireland, are the result of a lava flow along the northern coast of the island.*

33 *The greenness of the gentle velvety hills around Kilkullen, not far from the town of Kildare, is highlighted by the austere stone crosses in a small cemetery.*

Ashford Castle stands out amid the greenery of Connemara like an austere fortress decorated with towers and crenellated battlements which is mirrored in the waters of Lough Corrib. The castle was recently transfrmed into a hotel whose rooms contain authentic masterpieces of art and antique

furniture. The guests at Ashford are made to feel at home in an elegant and refined atmosphere in which even the simplest daily actions are experienced as pleasant events.

36 *The county of Kildare still contains many traces of those ancient peoples and adventurers who dominated Ireland before A.D. 100. The photograph shows the fortified Kilkea Castle.*

37 *Perched on a rocky promontory along the northern coast of the island, one can still see the grey walls of Dunluce Castle. Built in the 14th century, this castle has been uninhabited since 1641.*

One of Ireland's most famous castles is Adare Manor in county Limerick. This 19th-century stately home has recently been transformed into a welcoming and exclusive hotel with a private golf course and hunting reserve. The guests of Ardare Manor can admire the vast garden with its

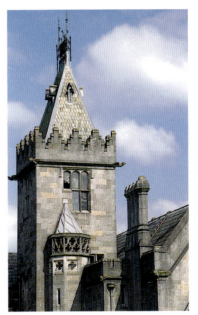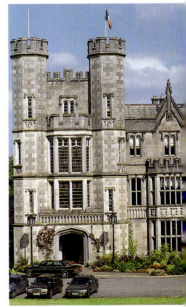

many flower beds and hedges. The courteous and relaxed atmosphere enables guests to spend some unforgettable days as they discover the pleasures of an Irish welcome and Irish cooking.

Facing the ocean

Travelling along the Irish Coast is equivalent to entering a world of marvels: endless stretches of greenery alternate with steep fjords which plunge down to the sea and deserted beaches contrast with wild moors constantly lashed by the wind. From the cliffs, especially when the low and damp mist clears, one can admire the most spectacular views of the Atlantic Ocean. On cool days when the sky is clear, the blue of the sea becomes darker and deeper and highlights the clear dividing line between the rocky cliff walls and the foaming brine as well as the contours of the inland hills.

40-41 top *The Donegal coast, in northwestern Ireland, is still extraordinarily wild.*

41 bottom *The Cliffs of Moher, dizzying and imposing, define County Clare in the west.*

42-43 *Fanad Head stretches out from the northern coast of Donegal.*

Romantic and lonely beaches are scattered all around the Irish coastline. Sometimes they are small crescents of sand hidden in bays which can only be reached from the sea and at times they are long stretches of fine sand which are periodically covered at high tide. Despite the mild air temperature, the water of the Atlantic is rather cold and only the more hardy visitors go for a swim. Such a deserted coastline under an often cloudy sky, makes the viewer very conscious of the beauty of nature and may lead him to contemplate on how the character of this island people, at times harsh and introverted and at times open and cheerful, may have been influenced by the place in which they live.

44 *The beaches of Wexford Bay are particularly beautiful and are very popular with tourists.*

45 *The Dingle peninsula, in the south-western part of the island, extends 25 miles into the Atlantic ocean.*

46-47 *There are many charming areas in Donegal: long deserted beaches, wild mountain valleys and fascinating nature reserves which have not been affected by human intrusion.*

The untamed side of Ireland

48 *The impressive cliffs of Moher stretch for more than five miles between Liscannor and Dolin, rising vertically to a height of more than 600 feet.*

49 Ocean winds lash the high rocky
cliffs of Moher and the roaring sea
thunders into the sandstone gorges of
this imposing stretch of coast.

50-51 *The Aran Islands emerge from the sea in front of Galway Bay. The three islands of Inishmore, Inishmaan and Inisheer consist almost exclusively of compact rock and stones and are like three uneven humps on the surface of the water.*

52-53 *The Aran Islands possess their own special primitive charm. Celtic culture and language still survive here and the inhabitants' rhythm of life is dictated by nature and is very similar to that of their forefathers.*

Irish silence and solitude

54 *While driving along deserted stretches of road, even in the wilder parts of Donegal, it is quite common to come across small wayside shrines. It was in A.D. 432 that St. Patrick laid the foundations of the Christain faith in this island.*

55 *A small cemetery near Kilcullen, in county Kildare, which, alongside the more recent gravestones, also contains stone crosses dating back to the Middle Ages.*

56-57 *Thanks to frequent rains, the Dingle peninsula is very rich in green meadows and grazing land.*

Wild Donegal

58-59 *Green hills, tilled fields, and lonely farms — this is a characteristic view of the Irish countryside in Donegal where many of the isolated houses still have thatched roofs.*

60-61 *View of the green countryside which slopes gently down to the sea. Donegal still retains ancient Gaelic traditions and the ancestral Irish language dating back to Celtic rule.*

The city on a human scale

Ireland remained isolated for centuries from the military and political upheavals of Europe. The Roman legions were kept so busy defending the Scottish border that they never invaded Ireland. Thus, Ireland did not have any important Roman cities which, in many other European states, formed the nuclei for later urban growth. With the Celts, Ireland continued to be divided into isolated tribal areas scattered over the inland plateaux. Only after the arrival of the Vikings, and later, the Normans, was there a development of trade with the continent. In fact, the Scandinavian invaders founded a number of coastal settlements, which later grew to become towns. These ports, which were fortified and enlarged by the Normans, became important mercantile ports of call, while the areas of the inner valleys still retained a predominantly agricultural way of life.

62 top The Customs House, designed by James Gandon, is considered one of the best examples of neo-classical architecture in Dublin.

62 bottom Ancient Dublin developed in a wide valley overlooking the sea along the banks of the Liffey River.

63 Behind the houses of Cobh, the port in Cork Bay which serves the city of Cork, is the beautiful cathedral of St. Colman, whose original construction dates from 14th century.

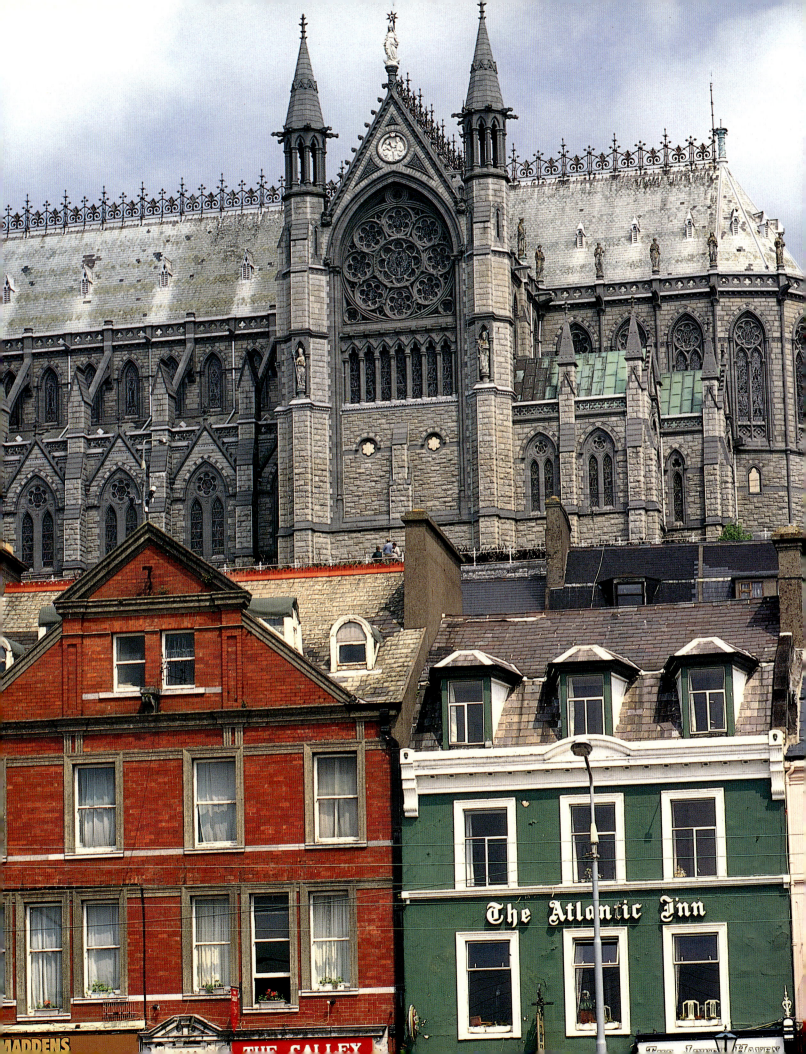

The Atlantic Inn

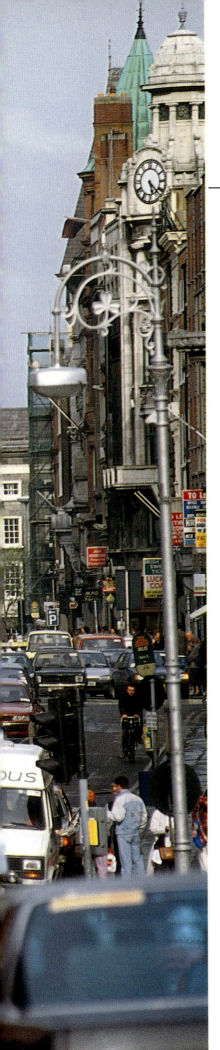

A friendly capital city

The present aspect of Dublin results from the period of marvellous town planning development which started in the 18th century, when the wide streets of O'Connell, Upper Merrion, and Baggot were established. During that period, a great number of bridges were built on the Liffey River, wide squares were planned, and numerous buildings in the Georgian style were erected. In some neighbourhoods, wide avenues, palaces decorated with columns, and the wrought-iron street lamps remind Dubliners of that much-debated period of prosperity that occurred under British rule. In the last decades of this century, Dublin has seen an impressive and unstoppable growth. In the sixties, advocates of urban development replaced entire residential neighbourhoods with offices and commercial palaces. The courageous work of restoration recovered the delicate beauty of the decorative plasters, the thin wrought-iron decorations, and those typical frames of Dubliner doors gracefully decorated with fanlights.

66 top *On a window near the entrance to a Dublin pub is the name of the most well known and popular Irish beer — Guinness.*

66 bottom *Stalls full of flowers brighten the crossroads and the pavements of the most fashionable Dublin neighbourhoods.*

67 top *The typical Doors of Dublin stand out in Merrion Square because they are framed by lively colours, white columns, and neoclassical friezes.*

67 bottom *In spite of uncontrolled building, some areas of the capital have still kept a provincial and even rural appearance.*

68-69 *A modern shopping centre still retains the charm of Irish life.*

The capital boasts one of the most well known circles of ingenious artists, such as Jonathan Swift, Sean O'Casey, Oscar Wilde, and James Joyce himself, whose most famous novel was set here. It is true that many Dubliners hope, at the bottom of their hearts, to establish themselves as poets and writers. Since

the abolition of censorship and since the position of the church became less severe, many young people, today more than ever, meet again in Grafton Street. They are dressed according to modern and often extravangant fashion.

72 top *St. Patrick's Cathedral, opened in 1192, is a beautiful Gothic structure that is dominated by a powerful, square-based tower.*

72 middle *The stately columns at the entrance to the National Museum overlook Merrion Street; inside, artifacts of great historical value are kept.*

72 bottom *The building which today houses the Irish Bank was built in 1729 to house the Irish Parliament.*

73 *Upon its foundation, made by the Danes, Christ Church Cathedral underwent several different expansions during the Norman period and was partially rebuilt in 1870.*

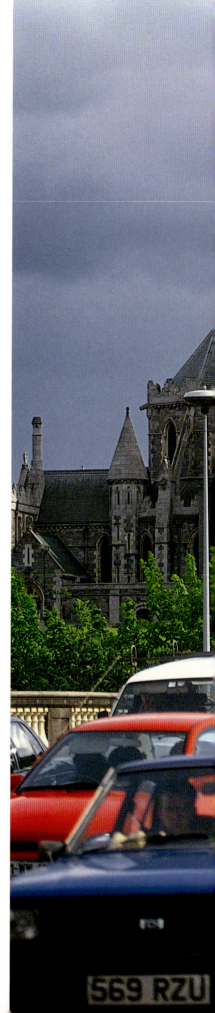

The castle of Dublin overlooks the capital from the promontory upon which it was built between 1202 and 1220. The medieval town developed around it, and for many centuries it was the symbol of British rule in Irish history. Most of the structure today goes back to the 18th century; the Record Tower, situated in the inner courtyard of the castle, is the only remains of the ancient Norman

fortress. Compared with the external architecture, the most interesting areas of the building are the interiors; St. Patrick's Hall, seventy-six feet long and thirty-six feet high, is the site for the installation ceremony for Irish presidents. The hall shows all its beauty in the fine panel decorations adorning the high ceiling, in the friezes, and in the stuccos on the walls. Even the other rooms are enriched with mirrors, golden columns, wonderful carpets, and elegant furniture; these rooms are employed by the government for formal meetings and State functions.

When evening falls, Dublin takes on a new atmosphere. The capital does not lose its liveliness and good mood, but the points of reference are shifted because of the rowdy groups of people — from the pedestrian precinct of Grafton Street to the terraces of the Abbey Theatre, from the arcades to the tables of one of the numerous pubs. Above all, the pub represents the most pleasant meeting place, the right spot to spend hours with friends over pints of stout or many small glasses of Irish whisky.

80-81 *With its shallow dome the Four Courts, seat of the Irish High and Supreme Courts, is one of the landmarks of Dublin. Originally built at the end of the 18th century, it was restored externally after the civil war of 1921-22.*

Indomitable Cork

Because of its lucky position on the coast and its commercial liveliness, Cork breathes continental air even if the town has always retained the proud independence that, in the 20th century, earned it the name "Rebel City." The first settlement, founded by St. Finbar in the sixth century, was built on a marshy strip between two branches of the Lee River that today are canals. The name "Cork" comes from a Gaelic word meaning water meadow or marshland. The old town centre of today still occupies the plain along the river, while the residential areas, situated on both banks, are arranged as an amphitheatre around it. Cork is the second city in the Republic of Ireland, and it boasts an efficient port, which, together with the nearby dock of Cobh, provided an economic boon to the people and to surrounding counties.

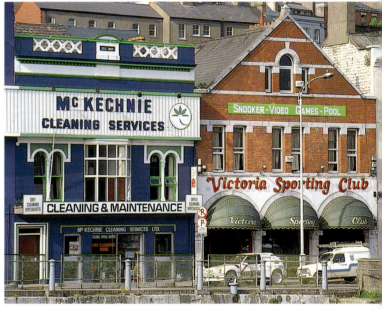

84-85 Cork is a busy centre on the southern coast, although it has no more than 150,000 inhabitants.

86-87 Beautiful wrought-iron decorations provide the finishing touch to the roof of the cathedral in Cobh, a seaport built near the mouth of the Lee River.

Colourful and secluded

Dingle is a lively little town situated in a small valley surrounded by graceful hills and directly facing Dingle Bay. Some time ago, its port was somewhat important because it was the landing place of ships coming from Spain. Today, the small fleet anchored at the wharf is used daily by fishermen. The town is the destination of a limited number of tourists and, for the time being, is not exceedingly crowded; visitors are allured by the beauty of the place, by the good, fresh fish served in the local restaurants, and by the sincere welcome of the inhabitants. Dingle is a very good starting point for a sightseeing tour of the wonderful surrounding landscape — a marvellous sequence of beaches, hills, and expanses of heath following one another on one of the most charming peninsulas of the western coast.

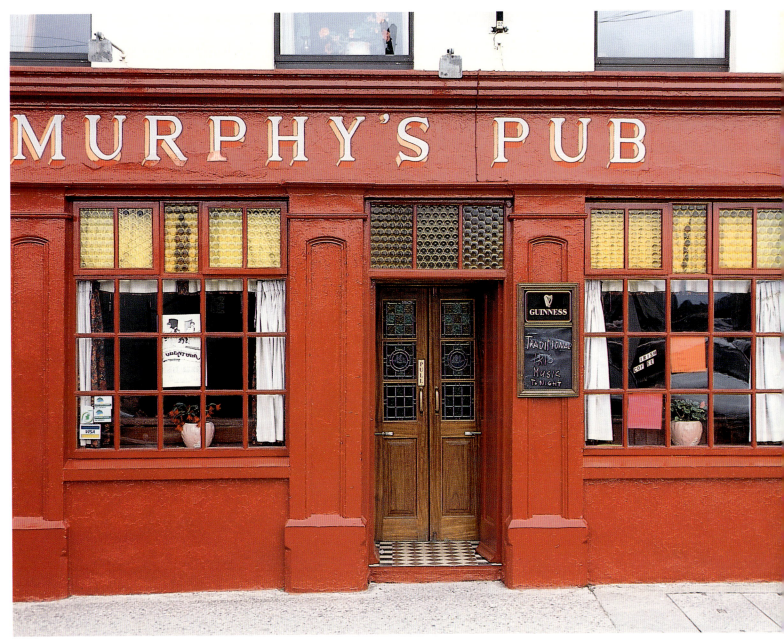

The divided city

90 Belfast Town Hall, built between the end of the 19th century and the beginning of the present century, appears in a sumptuous Renaissance style, with a large tower, 160 feet high and surmounted by a copper dome.

91 *In spite of the rapid industrial growth of the last century, which made the town into one of the major ports of call in the United Kingdom, Belfast still offers elegant buildings, wide avenues, and residential areas surrounded by parks and gardens.*

92-93 *Stormont, on the outskirts of Belfast, is the parliament building of Ulster. Built in the style of Buckingham Palace, it is the symbol of the British presence in Northern Ireland.*

A Celtic stronghold

The Irish people have succeeded in retaining their own autonomous cultural roots that date back to pre-Christian invaders from central Europe and have remained almost unchanged in spite of unsettling historical events and a long English rule. In the capital and in other, more industrialized towns, the signs of economic progress and of the social transformations that have accompanied the "boom" of the seventies are very clear.

New generations share an attitude of emancipation, and a certain freedom from custom appears to have relieved some of the pressure of strict moral and religious principles. Irish society, however, remains basically rural, tied to the rhythms of an often adverse and ungrateful land, to the religious rites handed down since St. Patrick, and to festivals commemorating past deeds of Celtic heroes. In some areas, time seems to have slackened its unrelenting pace; in the district known as *An Gaeltacht*, that peculiar Irish language, so rich in harmonious and untranslatable expressions, is still spoken.

94 top *A large and attentive audience watches an exciting race in Curragh.*

94 bottom *Most Irishmen assiduously haunt the pubs, where they meet to talk and drink good pints of beer.*

95 *Small thatched cottages are still found in many areas in Ireland.*

Land of the poets

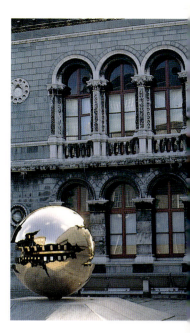

Trinity College, founded by Elizabeth I in 1592 for the Protestant middle classes of the day, soon became an important cultural centre, shaping many renowned writers and poets. The sober façade of the University building is embellished by a unique clock, whose blue dial appears surprisingly bright in direct

sunlight. Inside, there is a wide, cobblestone courtyard, where the austere theatre known as Examination Hall, and the beautiful chapel, both dating back to the 18th century, are located. Here, you can admire the original library, where the Book of Kells, the wonderful copy of the Gospels, decorated and handwritten by the monks during the ninth century, is displayed. Since its founding, Trinity College has become the spiritual centre for many Irish poets and playwrights and still today is a meeting place of teachers and students.

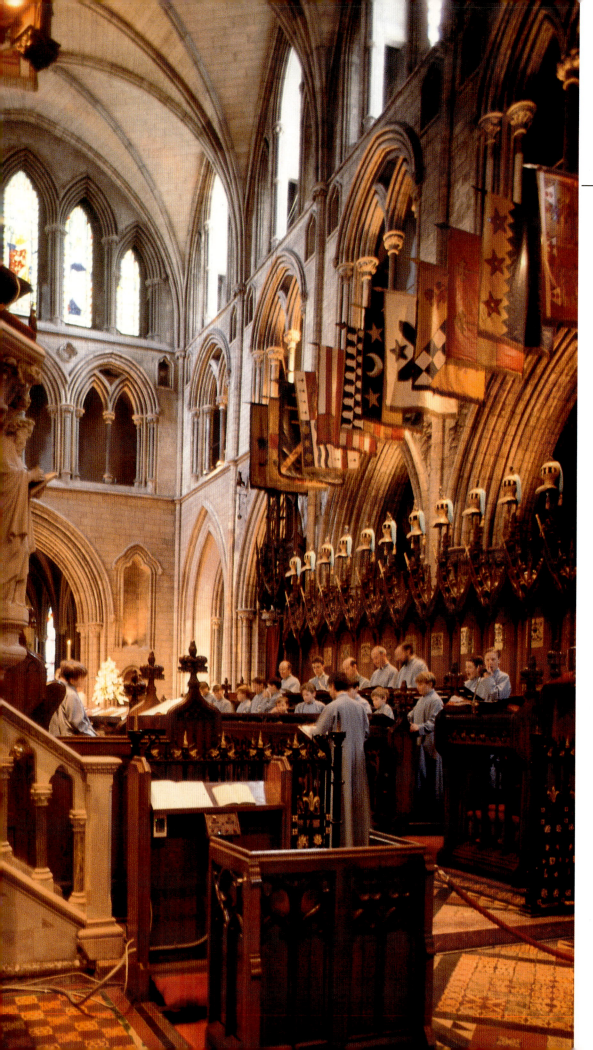

Faith and hope

St. Patrick's Cathedral dates back to the 12th century and has subsequently been enlarged and altered. Only toward the middle of the 19th century did the cathedral recover its former magnificence, thanks to restoration efforts subsidized by the Guinness family. St. Patrick contains several funerary monuments and memorial tablets, among them, Jonathan Swift's, dean of the church from 1712 to 1745. The inside is designed in a pleasant Gothic style with multi-coloured glass walls commemorating Biblical characters and events.

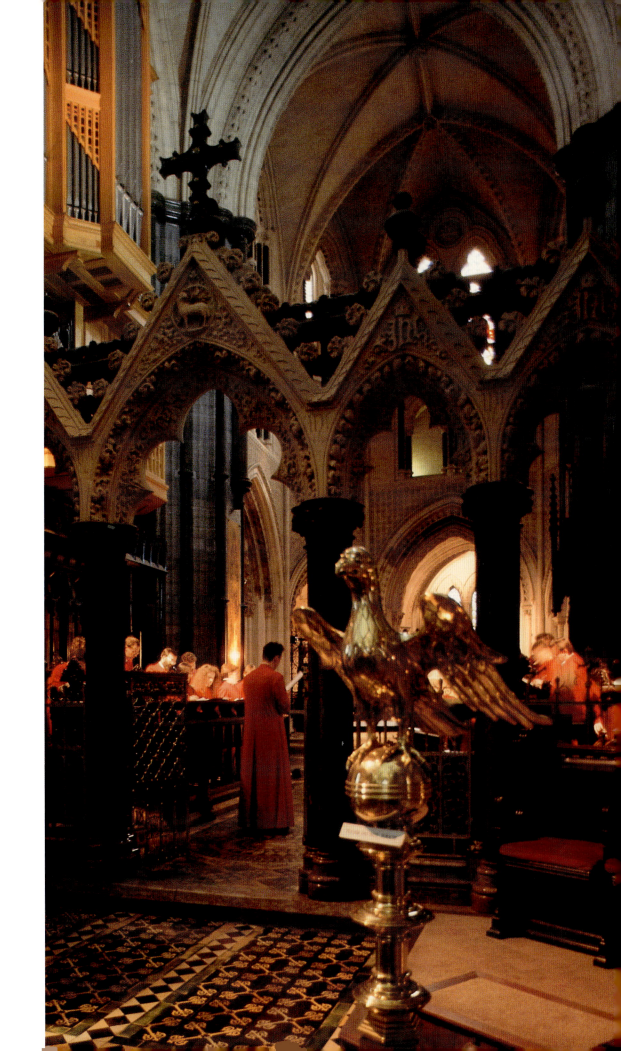

"Slainte!" — a toast

100 *Most pubs in Dublin still retain the traditional furniture, shunning bright lights and modern fixtures.*

100 top *Women have been allowed to enter pubs freely for only the past few decades; once these public premises had separate little rooms or provided screens in order to offer hospitality to the ladies at a proper distance from inquisitive looks.*

101 bottom *The usual drinks in Ireland are beer, which is directly drawn into the tankards, and the amber-coloured Irish whisky, pure and light because it is distilled three times and aged for a long time.*

Rural customs

The rhythm of life in the Irish countryside does not resemble the frantic activity of a modern and industrialized continental farm. In many areas, it is possible to till the land, and the only economic resource for some is still the breeding of horses. In fact, in many towns in Kerry, squares are periodically enlivened by a number of stockbreeders and farmers who, during these markets, negotiate the sale or the purchase of the best animals. On the contrary, the famous ponies, so appreciated and well known all over the world because of their temperament, their physical resistance, and a certain toughness, are from Connemara. Even though these horses are reared on decidedly barren grazing grounds, it is not rare to meet farmers who own animals of good quality, suitable even for shows.

104-105 *Some areas in the Irish countryside are poor and inhospitable, and many remote farms survive only on the food provided by their fields.*

105 top *Many farmers of the western counties extract peat from the marshlands. When dried, it will be used for fuel.*

106-107 *Silence and solitude are ever present with the people who live in the wildest and most desolate areas of the country.*

108-109 *About eighty per cent of Irish barley is used to produce local beers, divided between lager and bitter, while, for Guinness, the variety is called "stout."*

A respect for the ocean

The Irish are not a seafaring people, even though their country is surrounded by water. They have caught fish from the sea for centuries, during periods of famine, but the fragile small boats and motor trawlers have never allowed the fishermen to advance far into the stormy and unstable ocean. Better equipped modern fleets were established in the 20th century.

Solitary
pastimes

Ireland is a green, relaxing island. Irishmen find the right rhythm for their everyday activities — never too frenetic, because for them, time neither slows down nor speeds up its passing. Hobbies and pastimes are often solitary ones, among the velvet hills under a sky sometimes clear, sometimes leaden.

112 *During a break, two students at Trinity College play a friendly game of croquet on the campus lawn.*

113 top *Ireland is very rich in water; rivers, lakes, and streams offer many choices for those who love fishing.*

113 bottom *The country has considerable facilities for golfers. The golf courses are often situated in parks and in the gardens of residential castles.*

114-115 *Along the western coastline, the small sailing boats have many natural landing places at their disposal as they return from the open sea.*

A sporting heart

Besides the most common sports, in Ireland there are some that are practised exclusively on the island, probably dating back to ancient competitions among Celtic tribes. They are mostly amateur sports, giving rise to exciting local tournaments with a large and faithful following of spectators. Gaelic football is played above all in the county of Kerry, home of the best

players. This sport is an Irish mixture of football, soccer, and rugby: the players are allowed to grab hold of the ball with their hands and kick it or punch it; however, the rules are vague and continually changed, so most of the play is improvised. On the whole, Gaelic football is spectacular when a certain technique is used — some players are able to run while continuously passing the ball from their foot to their hand and vice versa.

118 *The most important football matches are often preceded by parades.*

118-119 *Flags bearing the colours of international countries and of the local teams wave in the stadium packed with people, as supporters sing the team anthem.*

Cheers and colours for the Irish teams

Ireland is a country of sportsmen, champions, first-rate teams, and gamblers. Although soccer is played at the highest levels, it is not the national sport. Other competitions, similar to soccer, have been practised since ancient times. In fact, Gaelic football and hurling are followed by a large audience, and fierce and colourful supporters cheer for their champions on Sundays from the crowded stadium. Rugby, tennis, golf, and, of course, horseback riding are also popular. Besides the competitions and tournaments among teams, Ireland offers the tourist several possibilities for turning their stay into an active holiday. Excellent golf courses are available all over the country, while if you want to enjoy horseback riding, you have much to choose from, with first-rate riding schools available everywhere and providing good trainers.

However, the true Irish national sport is hurling, practiced on the grassy grounds of the island since ancient times, when the ferocious barbarians challenged one other to similar competitions, which lasted several days. The rules are quite simple, and the sport is spectacular and exciting. The two teams are formed by fifteen players. Each player is supplied with a netless stick similar to that used to play hockey. The ball is one to two inches in diameter and is made of thread tightly rolled around a cork core and covered with leather. The aim of the play is to throw the ball between the goalposts of the opposing team; it may be hit with the hand, the feet, or, of course, with the mallet. Offensive and defensive actions are very quick; the most skillful players are able to run for several yards while bouncing the ball with their stick.

120 and 121 middle *Quickness and physical strenght are required for players to become champions in the sport of hurling.*

121 top and bottom *In a Gaelic football match, the two teams contend furiously to catch the ball.*

Passions and bets

The Irish people feel a passionate love for horses, together with a natural ability for riding and taking care of these animals. Horse races and all their relevant shows are very common, and they generally attract large crowds of spectators. Besides the more or less friendly competitions that take place in many small towns in the counties, Ireland boasts some of the most important and world-famous equestrian events. The "mother country" of horse racing is Curragh, a vast grassy plain in County Kildare, the heart of Irish competitive riding and the theatre of numerous classic competitions: the 1,000 and 2,000 Guineas, the Irish Guinness Oaks, and the Sweeps Derby.

124-125 *Horse racing is a mixture of different elements, and it provides a unique chance to meet Irish people of all ranks. The strong emotions restrained during most of the race explode in the final lap, when horses are spurred by jockeys in the finishing stretch. Then the crowd lets go with shouts of joy or cries of dismay. The 1,000 Guineas race is one of the classic equestrian events; horses and jockeys come from all over island to participate.*

126 *The most important equestrian event in Ireland, the Dublin Horse Show, has taken place in Dublin for more than a century.*

127 *On the day of the horse race in August, on the green, grassy mantle at Anglesea Stadium in Dublin, the packs used in fox hunting are shown before the equestrian event.*

Photo Credits:

All photographs were taken by Giulio Veggi, with the following exceptions:

Allstock/Zefa: Page 110, top left.

Cotton Caulson/Grazia Neri: Pages 106-107; 108-109.

Nino Cirani/Stradella: Pages 90; 91.

Dolci/Focus Team: Page 105 bottom.

Klaus D. Francke/Bilderberg/Grazia Neri: Page 26.

G.P. Reichell/Apa Photo Agency: Pages 104; 110 top right; 114-115.

Angelo Tondini/Focus Team: Pages 95; 110-111.

Michael Yamashita/Grazia Neri: Pages 92-93; 102; 103; 126; 127.